The Chalmers

by Iain Gray

Lang**Syne**

PUBLISHING

WRITING *to* REMEMBER

Lang**Syne**

PUBLISHING

WRITING *to* REMEMBER

Strathclyde Business Centre
120 Carstairs Street, Glasgow G40 4JD
Tel: 0141 554 9944 Fax: 0141 554 9955
E-mail: info@scottish-memories.co.uk
www.langsyneshop.co.uk

Designed by Dorothy Meikle
Printed by Thomson Litho, East Kilbride
© Lang Syne Publishers Ltd 2006
ISBN 1-85217-223-1
ISBN 978-1-85217-223-7

The Chalmers

Chapter one:

Origins of Scottish surnames

by George Forbes

It all began with the Normans.

For it was they who introduced surnames into common usage more than a thousand years ago, initially based on the title of their estates, local villages and chateaux in France to distinguish and identify these landholdings, usually acquired at the point of a bloodstained sword.

Such grand descriptions also helped enhance the prestige of these arrogant warlords and generally glorify their lofty positions high above the humble serfs slaving away below in the pecking order who only had single names, often with Biblical connotations as in Pierre and Jacques.

The only descriptive distinctions

among this peasantry concerned their occupations, like Pierre the swineherd or Jacques the ferryman.

The Normans themselves were originally Vikings (or Northmen) who raided, colonised and eventually settled down around the French coastline.

They had sailed up the Seine in their longboats in 900AD under their ferocious leader Rollo and ruled the roost in north east France before sailing over to conquer England, bringing their relatively new tradition of having surnames with them.

It took another hundred years for the Normans to percolate northwards and surnames did not begin to appear in Scotland until the thirteenth century.

These adventurous knights brought an aura of chivalry with them and it was said no damsel of any distinction would marry a man unless he had at least two names.

The family names included that of Scotland's great hero Robert De Brus and his compatriots were warriors from families like the De Morevils, De Umphravils, De Berkelais, De Quincis, De Viponts and De Vaux.

As the knights settled the boundaries of their vast estates, they took territorial names, as in Hamilton, Moray, Crawford, Cunningham, Dunbar, Ross, Wemyss, Dundas, Galloway, Renfrew, Greenhill, Hazelwood, Sandylands and Church-hill.

Other names, though not with any obvious geographical or topographical features, nevertheless derived from ancient parishes like Douglas, Forbes, Dalyell and Guthrie.

Other surnames were coined in connection with occupations, castles or legendary deeds. Stuart originated in the word steward, a prestigious post which was an integral part of any large medieval household. The same applied to Cooks, Chamberlains, Constables and Porters.

Borders towns and forts - needed in

areas like the Debateable Lands which were constantly fought over by feuding local families - had their own distinctive names; and it was often from them that the resident groups took their communal titles, as in the Grahams of Annandale, the Elliots and Armstrongs of the East Marches, the Scotts and Kerrs of Teviotdale and Eskdale.

Even physical attributes crept into surnames, as in Small, Little and More (the latter being 'beg' in Gaelic), Long or Lang, Stark, Stout, Strong or Strang and even Jolly.

Mieklejohns would have had the strength of several men, while Littlejohn was named after the legendary sidekick of Robin Hood.

Colours got into the act with Black, White, Grey, Brown and Green (Red developed into Reid, Ruddy or Ruddiman). Blue was rare and nobody ever wanted to be associated with yellow.

Pompous worthies took the name Wiseman, Goodman and Goodall.

Words intimating the sons of leading figures were soon affiliated into the language as in Johnson, Adamson, Richardson and Thomson, while the Norman equivalent of Fitz (from the French-Latin 'filius' meaning 'son') cropped up in Fitzmaurice and Fitzgerald.

The prefix 'Mac' was 'son of' in Gaelic and clans often originated with occupations - as in MacNab being sons of the Abbot, MacPherson and MacVicar being sons of the minister and MacIntosh being sons of the chief.

The church's influence could be found in the names Kirk, Clerk, Clarke, Bishop, Friar and Monk. Proctor came from a church official, Singer and Sangster from choristers, Gilchrist and Gillies from Christ's servant, Mitchell, Gilmory and Gilmour from servants of St Michael and Mary, Malcolm from a servant of Columba and Gillespie from a bishop's servant.

The rudimentary medical profession was represented by Barber (a trade which also once included dentistry and surgery) as well as Leech or Leitch.

Businessmen produced Merchants, Mercers, Monypennies, Chapmans, Sellers and Scales, while down at the old village watermill the names that cropped up included Miller, Walker and Fuller.

Other self explanatory trades included Coopers, Brands, Barkers, Tanners, Skinners, Brewsters and Brewers, Tailors, Saddlers, Wrights, Cartwrights, Smiths, Harpers, Joiners, Sawyers, Masons and Plumbers.

Even the scenery was utilised as in Craig, Moor, Hill, Glen, Wood and Forrest.

Rank, whether high or low, took its place with Laird, Barron, Knight, Tennant, Farmer, Husband, Granger, Grieve, Shepherd, Shearer and Fletcher.

The hunt and the chase supplied Hunter, Falconer, Fowler, Fox, Forrester, Archer and Spearman.

The renowned medieval historian Froissart, who eulogised about the romantic deeds of chivalry (and who condemned Scotland as being a poverty stricken waste-land), once sniffily dismissed the peasantry of his native France as the jacquerie (or the jacques-without-names) but it was these same humble folk who ended up overthrowing the arrogant aristocracy.

In the olden days, only the blueblooded knights of antiquity were entitled to full, prop-er names, both Christian and surnames, but with the passing of time and a more egalitari-an, less feudal atmosphere, more respectful and worthy titles spread throughout the popu-lace as a whole.

Echoes of a far distant past can still be found in most names and they can be borne with pride in commemoration of past genera-tions who fought and toiled in some capacity or other to make our nation what it now is, for good or ill.

Chapter two:

Martyrs of the Covenant

Proud bearers of the surname of Chalmers, or Chambers, may be pleasantly surprised to learn that their name has distinctly regal connotations, stemming as it does from the trusted office of chamberlain, who was in charge of the 'chamber', or exchequer, into which royal revenues were paid.

Of Anglo-Saxon origin, variations include Chaumers, Chamber, and Chamberlain, with Chalmers being the Scottish form of the common English form of Chambers.

Both names, however, have flourished in Scotland over the centuries.

The process whereby nobles paid money into the royal exchequer in return for the lands they held was known in Latin as paying 'in cameran', while the 'camerarius', or 'chamberlain', was in charge of this often complex process.

A grandly named Herbertus, who held lands in both Lanarkshire and Ayrshire, is recorded as the Camerarius Regis Scotiae, or Great Chamberlain of Scotland, during the reign from 1124 to 1153 of Scotland's David I.

One of his descendants, James Chalmers of Gadgirth, was a fiery Protestant reformer whose zeal was much admired and remarked on by the great father of the Reformation John Knox.

Chalmers even went as far as berating the regent Mary of Guise herself in an infamous public confrontation in 1558.

A Robert de la Chaumbre is recorded in 1296, while an Alexander of Chamour is recorded in 1461 in Aberdeen, and it is in Aberdeenshire that the families of Chalmers of Balnacraig, Cults, and Albar flourished for centuries, while there were also prominent families of the name in Ayrshire.

In addition to the Protestant reformer James Chalmers of Gadgirth, a number of Chalmers also figure prominently in the annals of

Scotland's often bitter religious history.

Robert Chalmers was one of five men from the parish of Shotts, in Lanarkshire, who were among 201 Covenanter prisoners who drowned while being transported to Barbados to be sold as slaves after being captured at the battle of Bothwell Brig.

A National Covenant, pledging defence of the Presbyterian religion, had been signed in the Greyfriars Kirk, in Edinburgh, in February of 1638.

Copies were circulated throughout the length and breadth of Scotland, and the hundreds of ordinary folk who signed it, such as Robert Chalmers, were known as Covenanters.

Episcopal rule was foisted on the Scottish Church following the Restoration of Charles II in 1660, and ministers who refused to abide by this were deprived of their parishes.

The Covenanters rose in rebellion in November of 1666 and many of the prisoners taken were tortured and hanged.

Victory for the Covenanters came at the

battle of Drumclog in June of 1679, only to be followed a few short weeks later by defeat at the battle of Bothwell Brig, near Hamilton.

Nearly 800 Covenanters were killed, and 1,400 taken prisoner. Kept for several weeks in open cages in the Greyfriars Kirkyard, those who agreed to sign a bond for future 'good behaviour' were released, but by November of 1679, a number of prisoners, including Robert Chalmers, still remained.

The authorities decided to sell them as slaves on the plantations of Barbados, and 250 of them, including Chalmers, were packed aboard the Crown of London, which set sail from Leith on November 27.

Battling ferocious winter storms, the Crown of London sailed up the east coast of Scotland, finally being forced to anchor for safety off the headland of Scarva Taing, near the Mull Head of Deerness, in Orkney.

Disaster struck as the ship's anchor snapped in the raging torrents and the vessel was driven onto rocks. The crew managed to escape, but the captain ordered that the hatches securing the prisoners below decks remained locked.

About fifty prisoners did manage to make it to land, however, but as they attempted to claw their way to safety up the steep cliff face they were callously pushed back down onto the jagged rocks and into the raging sea on the orders of the captain.

More than 200 bodies were later washed up on the Deerness coastline.

The uncompromising stance taken on matters of religion by Covenanting martyrs such as Robert Chalmers was also taken up in later centuries by Dr Thomas Chalmers, the preacher, theologian, and economist who was born in Anstruther, Fife, in 1780.

Regarded as the most influential preacher of the nineteenth century, he was appointed professor of divinity at Edinburgh University in 1843, and following what is known as the 'Disruption' of the Church of Scotland in 1843, he became a founder of the Free Church of Scotland and its first Moderator.

While there is a Chalmers family motto of 'Advance', and a crest of the head and neck of a lion, bearers of the name are also recognised as a sept, or branch, of the proud Clan Cameron, and any Chalmers of today who can trace a descent back to the ancient Cameron homeland of Lochaber are entitled to share in the clan's motto of 'Unite', its crest of a sheaf of five arrows, and adopt its tartan.

A rather curious tradition relates to how bearers of the surname Chalmers became a sept of the clan - a tradition that has its roots in the fact that many Scots, particularly the sons of noble families, entered the military service of successive French monarchs.

One of these was a Cameron who took the Latin name of Camerarius, or Camerario, as 'being more agreeable to the language of that country': in French, this translated as 'de la Chambre', or 'Chalmers/Chambers'.

When he returned to Scotland (although some sources state it was his son), the name was retained, and so was later founded the 'dynasty' of the Chalmers of Aberdeenshire.

This Chalmers link to Clan Cameron makes them heirs to a proud, but often bloody, tradition.

Chapter three:

For the Jacobite cause

Clan Cameron had for centuries held lands in the Lochaber region, mainly around Loch Lochy, and it was a Sir John de Cameron who in 1321 was one of the signatories of that resounding clarion call of Scotland's freedom known as the Declaration of Arbroath.

Ninety years later, the Camerons and their kinsfolk such as the Chalmers took part in one of the most savage battles on Scottish soil, the battle of Harlaw, fought on July 24, 1411.

Also known as the Battle of Red Harlaw because of the blood spilled, no side emerged victorious.

Donald MacDonald, 2nd Lord of the Isles, had mustered about 6000 of his best clansmen and burned Inverness after crossing to the mainland and marching up the Great Glen.

His strength swelled to 10,000 after other clansmen including Camerons,

Chattans, MacIntoshes, and MacLeods joined him. Promising them rich pickings, MacDonald marched them towards Aberdeen.

The Earl of Mar hastily assembled a force that included northeast lairds while the Provost of Aberdeen also raised men.

The opposing forces met just north of Aberdeen, and battle was joined shortly after the summer sun had risen.

The fearless and ferocious clansmen repeatedly charged the ranks of the Earl of Mar and his men, only to be cut down in swathes, but not before exacting their own toll in blood.

As the sun sank low in the west, both sides were exhausted and had to retire from the fray, leaving behind a battlefield littered with the corpses of at least 1000 clansmen and 600 of Mar's men.

Chalmerses were also among the Cameron kinsfolk who fought under the colours of Sir Ewen Cameron of Lochiel, 17th Chief of Clan Cameron, at the battle of Killiecrankie.

Following the 'Glorious Revolution' of

1688 that brought William of Orange and his wife Mary to the thrones of England and Scotland, John Graham of Claverhouse, Viscount Dundee, raised the Royal Standard in favour of the exiled Stuart monarch James VII and II.

Gathering a 2,500-strong force of clansmen that included a contingent from Clan Cameron, he engaged a 4000-strong government force under General Hugh Mackay of Scourie at the Pass of Killiecrankie on July 27, 1689.

Brave, but undisciplined, the clansmen fired off a volley of musket fire before throwing the muskets to the ground and rushing pell-mell down hill into Mackay's closely packed ranks.

The clansmen were mown down in their hundreds by the disciplined musket fire of Mackay's troopers, but not before inflicting equally heavy losses.

Both sides suffered terribly in the battle and the outcome proved to be inconclusive, but, fatally for the cause of the exiled Stuart king, 'Bonnie Dundee' died the next day from his wounds.

Jacobite unrest in Scotland intensified following the Hanoverian succession to the throne under George, Elector of Hanover, in 1714, and in September of the following year John, the 11th Earl of Mar, raised the Standard of James VIII and III, the 'Old Pretender', at Braemar.

Mar raised an impressive force that included Camerons under the leadership of John, the son of the 17th chief who had fought at Killiecrankie.

The Jacobite ranks were plagued by bad leadership and lack of a coherent strategy, however, and the cause was effectively lost following the battle of Sheriffmuir on November 13, after Mar lost the initiative by withdrawing north to Perth.

The Old Pretender landed at Peterhead in December, later travelling to Perth where he held a dispirited court for three weeks before departing for foreign shores, never to return.

It was Donald Cameron, known to posterity as 'the Gentle Lochiel', and whose father had fought for the Old Pretender, who let his heart rule his head and, against his better judgement, supported the doomed cause of the Young Pretender, Prince Charles Edward Stuart, during the abortive Jacobite Rising of 1745 to 1746.

The prince had landed on the small Outer Hebridean island of Eriskay on July 22, 1745, landing on the mainland at Loch nan Uamh three days later.

It was vital for him to receive the armed support of the powerful clan chiefs in his quest to restore the Royal House of Stuart to the throne, and one of his first visitors was the Gentle Lochiel.

Although Lochiel welcomed his prince with all due respect, he informed him that without an army at his back he should never have come.

The angry prince is said to have retorted: 'In a few days, with the few friends that I have, I will erect the royal standard and proclaim to the people of Britain that Charles Stuart is come over to claim the crown of his ancestors, to win it or perish in the attempt', adding that Lochiel could stay at home and learn the fate of his prince from the newspapers.

His Highland pride stung by this, Lochiel

replied: 'No! I will share the fate of my prince and so shall every man over whom nature or fortune has given me any power!'

The Jacobite Standard was raised a few weeks later, on August 19, at Glenfinnan, on Loch Shiel, and Lochiel and his 800 clansmen and kinsfolk were among the first to rally to it.

It is also known that Chalmers was a 'code-name' for many Camerons during the Rising, and they were destined to pay a bloody price for their support, however, when Jacobite hopes were dashed forever at the battle of Culloden, fought on Drummossie Moor, near Inverness, on April 16, 1746.

In what was the last major battle fought on British soil, hundreds of clansmen died on the battlefield while hundreds of others died later from their wounds and the brutal treatment of their government captors.

The Muster Roll for the Jacobite army records that four men of the name of Chalmers, including two ploughmen, served in the Forfarshire (Ogilvy's) Regiment, while Francis

Chalmers was a servant to Lord George Murray, the prince's Lieutenant General.

Charles Chalmers, a merchant from Edinburgh, served in Elcho and Balmerino's Lifeguards, while William Chalmers served under the colours of the Duke of Perth's Regiment and John Chalmers served with the Irish Picquets.

Less than a century later, bearers of the name of Chalmers were still to be found on the battlefield, and one of the most prominent of them was Major General Sir William Chalmers, of Glenericht, in Perthshire.

Born in 1787, he entered army service at the age of 16, and by the time of the battle of Waterloo in 1815 he was in command of a wing of the 52nd Foot.

A redoubtable warrior who was always found in the thick of battle, he is reckoned to have had nine horses killed or wounded under him during his military career – three of them at Waterloo alone.

Far from the battlefield, however, proud

bearers of the name of Chalmers and Chambers
have achieved distinction in a wide variety of
rather more peaceful pursuits.

Chapter four:

Men of letters

The names of Chalmers and Chambers figure significantly in the world of publishing and literature, not least the brothers William and Robert Chambers, sons of a Peebles cotton manufacturer, and who founded the famous *Chambers Journal* in 1832 and completed the equally famous *Chambers Encyclopaedia* in 1868.

The printer James Chalmers was the founder in 1746 of the *Aberdeen Journal*, while his son established the *Aberdeen Almanack* in 1771.

George Chalmers, meanwhile, who was born at Fochabers, in Morayshire, in 1742, was an antiquarian and controversial political writer whose many works include a history of Scotland and a series of biographical sketches of famous figures such as Daniel Defoe.

James Chalmers, born in Arbroath in 1782, but who settled in Dundee, was not only a bookseller, printer, and newspaper publisher, but also the inventor in 1834 of the adhesive postage stamp, while Alexander Chalmers was the Scots-born biographer and editor who wrote newspapers in London in addition to prefaces for new editions of English classics.

He is best known, however, for his monumental *General Biographical Dictionary*, published in thirty-two volumes between 1812 and 1817.

Patrick Chalmers was the Irish writer who, before his death in 1942, contributed to *Punch* magazine and wrote prolifically on a range of subjects that included field sports, horse racing, and deer stalking, while Floyd Chalmers, born in Ohio in 1898 but later settling in Canada, became a leading editor, publisher, and philanthropist.

On a rather gruesome note, James Chalmers was a Scottish missionary, born in Ardrishaig, who suffered the unfortunate fate of being eaten by cannibals in New Guinea.

William Chalmers, the son of a Scottish merchant who had settled in Sweden, became a director of the Swedish East India Company in 1783, and was appointed their representative in Canton, China.

He died in Gothenburg in 1811 and left a bequest for 'an industrial school', which is renowned today as Gothenburg's Chalmers University of Technology.

In the world of art, George Chalmers, who was born in Montrose in 1836 was an accomplished portrait painter, but is better known today for his landscapes such as *The Legend*, and *A Quiet Cup*, which can both be seen in Edinburgh's National Gallery, and *The End of the Harvest*, and *Running Water*.

In contemporary times, the Australian-born David Chalmers is one of the world's leading philosophers and author of the best selling *The Conscious Mind*.

In the world of sport, Stevie Chalmers, born in Glasgow in 1936, and who overcame meningitis at an early age, is one of the famous 'Lisbon Lions', who scored the winning goal for Celtic Football Club in the 1967 European Cup

Final in Lisbon against Inter Milan.

Chalmers, who joined Celtic in 1959, won five Scottish caps and, at the time of writing, holds the record of the club's fourth top goal scorer. His son, Paul, also played for Celtic.

On the rugby pitch, Craig Chalmers, born in 1968, is the former Scottish Rugby Union player for Melrose. A fly half, he was capped sixty times for his country, and represented both the British Lions and Scotland at international level.

In the world of broadcasting, Manchester born Judith Chalmers is a versatile popular British radio and television broadcaster who was honoured with an O.B.E. for her services in 1994.

In the legal world, David Chambers, known as David Chambers of Ormond, was a sixteenth century Scottish judge who had the onerous task during the reign from 1542 to 1567 of Mary, Queen of Scots, of compiling and publishing the Acts of the Scottish Parliament.

He appears to have taken time out from his labours, however, to become one of the conspirators who were involved in the murder of the queen's dissolute husband, Lord Darnley, in 1567.

On a rather more creative note, and in the world of contemporary music, Guy Chambers is the highly talented songwriter who has composed a string of hits for a number of artists, including Robbie Williams, collaborating with him as a writer and producer on five of his best-selling albums.